I See Your Light

AhneeKA

Copyright © 2014 by AhneeKA

All rights reserved. This book or any portion thereof
may not be reproduced or used in any manner whatsoever
without the express written permission of the author
except for the use of brief quotations in a book review.

Printed in the United States of America

First Printing, 2014

ISBN-13: 9781500209582
ISBN-10: 1500209589

Independently Published
www.AhneeKA.com
ankaAhneeKA@aol.com

*This book is dedicated to Abdel
Who unknowingly
Motivated me
To finally publish this book*

I See Your Light

AhneeKA

*You
Are An Amazing
Wondrous Person*

You Who Have Lived Through Such Trials

*You
Who Have Learned
To Build
Magnificent Barriers*

To Protect Your Heart

To Hide Your Light

Do You Know Your Soul Shines Through Nonetheless?

I See Your Light

I Know Your Beauty

Do You?

The Angels Celebrated
The Day
You
Were Born

Another Beautiful Soul

To Lighten The World

*Another Bright Heart
To Shine Hope
For Those
Who Have Forgotten
Their Magnificence*

For Those Who Have Learned to Build Magnificent Barriers Instead

*To Hide Their Light
Because They Think
No One
Wants To See It*

I See Your Light

*I See The Truth
Of Who You Are*

Do You Want To Know What I See?

I See Your Beauty Shining From the Inside Out

*I See
All The Amazing
And Wonderful Things
You Will Do
And Experience*

You Are A Leader

Guiding Others As You Would Like To Be Guided

You Are A Teacher

*Showing Others
How To Live Life
To Its Fullest*

You Are A Student

*Learning
And Remembering
How Magnificent
You Really Are*

*I See
Your Light

And It Warms
My Heart*

*I See
Your Kindness*

*And Know
I Could Count On You
If I Was In Need*

*I See
You Living
Your Absolutely
Positively
Best Life ever*

Because...

*YOU See
Your Light
and Have The Courage
To Share
It with The World*

As Only You Can

Your Light Shines Most Brightly When You Remember...

*... To See Life
As An Adventure*

*With Wonderful Surprises
Around Every Bend*

*... That You
Are An Amazing Being*

*Who Can Do And Be
Anything You Choose*

... To Create Beautiful Thoughts

*... To Notice
The Good Things
In Your Life*

And Say Thank You

...That You Are So Much More Than You Think

... That All Your Answers Lie Within Your Own Heart

... And That Love

And Fear

Are The Only Real Choices

I Wish You Joy

And Love

And Peace

I See Your Light

I Celebrate Your Life

I Hope You Do Too!

www.AhneeKA.com

Made in the USA
Lexington, KY
02 June 2017